TALKING TO
SHADOWS

SOUTHERN MESSENGER POETS

Dave Smith, Series Editor

RON HOUCHIN

TALKING TO
SHADOWS

POEMS

LOUISIANA STATE UNIVERSITY PRESS ▌▌ BATON ROUGE

Published by Louisiana State University Press
www.lsupress.org

LSU Press Paperback Original

DESIGNER: *Mandy McDoanld Scallan*
TYPEFACE: *Whitman*

Grateful acknowledgment is due the editors of the following journals and venues
where some of these poems, sometimes in earlier versions, were originally pub-
lished: *Appalachian Heritage; Birmingham Poetry Review; Blue Lyra Review; Devilfish
Review; Dogs Singing: A Tribute Anthology* (Salmon Publishing); *Eyes Glowing at the
Edge of the Woods* (anthology, West Virginia University Press); *Pikeville Review; Pine
Mountain Sand & Gravel; Pine Mountain Sand & Gravel: The Dead* (special issue);
Potomac Review; Revolution John; Salmon: A Journey in Poetry (Salmon Publishing);
Stinging Fly (Ireland); *The Stony Thursday Book* (Ireland 2017); yourdailypoem.com.

Cover image: (Unsplash): Maarten Brakke

Library of Congress Cataloging-in-Publication Data

Names: Houchin, Ron, author.
Title: Talking to shadows : poems / Ron Houchin.
Description: Baton Rouge : Louisiana State University Press, [2020] |
    Series: Southern messenger poets
Identifiers: LCCN 2020009484 (print) | LCCN 2020009485 (ebook) | ISBN
    978-0-8071-7272-8 (paperback) | ISBN 978-0-8071-7435-7 (pdf) | ISBN
    978-0-8071-7436-4 (epub)
Subjects: LCGFT: Poetry.
Classification: LCC PS3558.O8345 T35 2020 (print) | LCC PS3558.O8345
    (ebook) | DDC 811/.54—dc23
LC record available at https://lccn.loc.gov/2020009484
LC ebook record available at https://lccn.loc.gov/2020009485

FOR ROGER *and* MARY HUNGATE

CONTENTS

TALKING TO SHADOWS

TALKING TO SHADOWS, NOVEMBER 1

they will wield power in the smallest ways . . .
—COLM TÓIBÍN

Early evening, the first lamps light
in dew on grass.
Before I've walked half the hill, they're there
among the streetlight's ellipsis,
the brocade of trees
trying to remember green, and the silence
that avoids saying
anything that might reach ears.

To speak to shadows is to remain still
in their reshaping the world.
Long limbs lengthen, slanting toward each other,
as if a hard wind pushes them over Earth.
A church steeple crosses the road,
only its chimes reaching the last of daylight.

CLEANING GLASSES

Standing at the mirror rubbing my eyeglasses
With an old washcloth one evening,
I saw my grandfather's fierce squint

Leering back at me and remembered
How unsettling it was when adults
In the family took off their spectacles

To make a point, to threaten punishment,
Or to sleep, and lost their familiar masks.
Without the friendly barrier of lenses,

Eyes looking at me with saurian suspicion
Held too much pink in the rims, and the skin
Seemed withdrawn from the world, overly naked.

If I came to in the cool of night and wandered
By any of their doors, I dared not stop and stare
At an alien body so cadaverous on a high bed.

I promised myself never to wear such things,
Become so strange, or grow complacent in time,
Then, one day, become familiar stranger to myself.

LITTLE DUTCH MILKMAID

(figurine, circa 1949)

One thing I saw more often in childhood
than crescent-moon bric-a-brac shelves
or milk glass pitchers sitting in bowls was you
bearing your small symmetry into the house.

Often I asked air about your wooden shoes,
the wings of your Flying Nun bonnet,
five dark pleats of your white apron,
and the duality of your pigtails.

Later, I imagined your hair parting, severe,
under that headgear and the tiny bucket,
at each end of a yoke, to be filled with milk,
water, tulips, or two thimblefuls

of something like sun exploding, bright
irony at the fission of fear and anger
of what we were becoming after a hot
war and the beginning of a cold one.

PHANTOM OF THE ALLEY

Anyone may stand, studying his part, gazing
out to sea at night, but he leaned
between trash bin and garage door, cigarette
smoke wreathing his head, as if counting
bricks, straining to see through fog a distant island,
or some light within. Whether he carried a sense
of placelessness to our alley or was restive,
smoking and running his lines, I never cared.
People squander silence disputing pointless matters.
Aunts and uncles wondered about him
when strolling little shops or folding towels
at their launderette. And we kids lay
each night in our huddled blankets, tuning
into dream with a cat's whisker for joy and mystery.
That alley was a stage, a place we could not just
pass through. Bricks visible from our fifth-floor
windows reflected more than sheen
and scattered puddles of rain. When I was ten,
I asked Mother about him. He was here
before I was, out there making each day's act
of wonder. Like a lost father, his face was harder
to see than blowing weeds in an abandoned field.

Everyone goes out at night for the other thing.
Alphonse for the annihilation of alcohol, looking
toward the first pint, the way a sunflower leans

toward sun, but gets into a taxi. Sherwood, in love
with misery first, Carol second, slips out to jam
with his band, Elroy and the Others, sings

"Oh, Carol" first thing. Beatrix for coffee, sits hours
in her neighborhood diner half-pretending to be
in a famous painting she had on a calendar

of nighthawks, all of whom leaned at a counter,
drinking coffee as if peaceably waiting for morning
to let them out. This doesn't help Bea,

so she hurls her heavy white mug across the tables
to bound off a wall of framed boxers' photos.
She's tossed out again onto the street but punches

Otto, the proprietor, in the gut when he drops
her on a bench. He pukes his last cup of coffee
near her sneakers. She walks home with no thought

but sleep. Alphonse and Sherwood snore through
their doors as Beatrix treads past to bed, happy
to stay out later, asleep already, dreaming sunflowers.

CATFISH CONTROLLING THE RIVER

Mayflies on thin reeds bob in water breeze,
their wings strumming chords of air
as they lift off.

Beneath leaden water, catfish legislate
currents, debating over the gray
weight on their backs.

Fishing hawks police the surface
for loafing sunfish. There never was
refuge in the river,

even as it spun me on its back in my black
inner tube. No alignment of minds in the meditation
of pole and line,

just deep, decorous waters and sparkling sun.
The congress of the river was ongoing,
and I was barely in the way.

SNAIL CHASING

First cousins to taste the shell, Marla and I hovered behind him
like gods behind a slow cyclist, as he crossed the sidewalk
in the sun. We could see the rhythm of his undulations, going
with as much velocity as he could muster. Sad how intention runs
often so far ahead of body. His was a coiled spring
that could not uncoil for rust. I couldn't resist swooping down,
seeing the fine ridges that make up his Fibonacci shell,
kneeling low so the late afternoon shown through,
seeing the tiny engine of his motor home. What miniature message
played in nerve endings, not quite a brain, in his head?
His stalk eyes erect, he searched the half-inch ahead for sudden
divots and ditches—and I did it! I licked the shell, sending
slow panic into his world and mine. What I heard with my ear
to the grain of the cement was what Marla and I could not know:
whether we were the king and queen of heaven, quick and cruel
as Nazis or just giants whose moving ways he could not understand,
that he might have worshipped, if his thin prayers could have made
it to our tremendous ears. Finally, all I know is that his body
was the tongue that licked the world with its worship.

WISDOM OF STARLINGS

I
know desire gives me wings;
attainment, just things. I want
to get up from this bed and walk
back to the war from home.
Two starlings: their heads disappear
in grass around the weeping pine.
Their wings, showing hundreds
of gold chevrons like flight badges
for each mile spent in the sky,
make me think of World War

II
They drop in one second
and flutter out the next.
Who knows by their anonymity,
if they're the same birds of the minute
before. Flashing around the town
like magicians, they clutter
the atmosphere with squawk and fluster.
Their multiplication in trees
reminds me that Irish farmers once
called them druids. Now there are

III

like splotches from an ink pen
that must be shook or dabbed
to keep scrawling. They show up
left when I look right. The day
would be a blanker page without their stain.
That they have been here much longer
than war soothes me, enabling these thoughts
of finishing this overdue letter that will
show up suddenly in your basket.
Even at so great a gulf, with wounds
like ours, we can know there are
only small distances, as the world
turns back to neighborhood.

HAUNTED BY DEAD DOGS

(for Art & Sadie)

Their heads down, walking stiff-shouldered
toward a door they can't remember is closed,
even their spirits need out to pee.

Like the best aspects of us, they're left
to nap on an island of folded blankets
down the hall.

If I were wealthy, I'd keep a Quonset hut
of memories for all the dogs
I've ever known.

Dobie, Trixie, Matty, Sadie, Teddy—
all their long-*e* sounds crying
at the end of the names we gave them,

like our wailing at the end of their lives.
I would gather them in from their plots
beside aluminum outbuildings in backyards,

from under special trees in the oak woods
outside of town. It would be a convention
of memory, a conference of elegies

like this one, perhaps, better left
unwritten— all their sweet old eyes
and gray muzzles lifted in half-round air,

at once yowling nostalgias for us
whom they miss more than
their own lives.

WINTER FEEDING

Water pipes froze, trailers burned, cold-weather
asthma killed, but now, early spring, still winter,
two yearling does stand beside the highway

in dull grass—thin, bedraggled, glimpses of
the forbidden, the ghosts of ghosts—my two
dead cousins with the same startled brown stare.

Each passing semi slaps wind against them
again like January. From the rearview
mirror, I am back in below-zero night

where one doe leans against a sapling,
the other curls on fallen pine needles,
their stomachs clenching emptiness,

neither thinking spring is just around
the corner. Through the curving of four lanes,
I watch in whichever of three mirrors

they still stand, to see their future. I want
to know that they didn't make it through
the rough winter feeding on the hearts

of pine cones, nubs of grass their hooves brought up
from packed snow, and the bark of wind-burned firs,
to be disassembled now by coal truck.

But this is all just language—they wait
at a rolling river of fast metal,
listening into the hollow of hills.

DISTANCE FROM THE DREAM SELF

No matter what he's doing on the tip
of the skyscraper,
balancing like a clown,
I put him there.

Looking over his shoulder,
I see his collar turned up, spiky, a way
of wearing it I've never tried. When he hauls
so maniacally on the oars, I hardly recognize him.

I know he's up to something I can't figure
out. Every time he turns around, he secrets
something under his coat.
It whimpers, its tail twitching.

I stood in the darkened room
waiting and no car lights came in
from outside as evening grayed,
then blackened into night. I stood

as if you would show up to talk,
explain things as you often did
in your *now-that-the-show-is-over-
here's-the-real-story* way. I knew

you probably could not come, unless
waiting in quiet dark is how haunting
begins. I didn't know what to do next,
so just stood as if my clothes would

fall off like leaves and I would be
asleep—a tree in the dead of winter.

THE LAST WINDOW ON THE ISLAND

It clouds with the thin light of uncounted hours,
daylong overcast or rain.
All weather hits this side as if the Atlantic
stays angry.

Names separated villages until famine,
flood, and plague erased all.
Help never came. Now the occasional
boat drifts by

leaving a wind-puffed plastic bag
or fast-food wrapper
to tumble over sleeping grasses.

It is a matter of faith, and it's not,
that a lone window still
stands with a cross heart and four panes,
none of which opens.

The window can only be gazed through,
like the trees, the people,
and laughter rubbed and smoothed away.

On one pane, rain beads and hangs
long.
On the second, dry ovals of spray
appear in each

accident of sun through clouds.
The third segment,
forgives, cracking diagonally
down its length.

The fourth's the first, oldest and wavy,
bejeweled by four
air bubbles, and stays clearest.

I think which is which matters only
if you were once
on this island and left or never were,
and still cannot get away.

(for Michael Heffernan)

HOW THE DEAD REMEMBER

Some nights they line up outside my window
like peeping toms.

Feeling their presence, I walk around the outside,
then look in, the way they do.

The chair where I like to sleep, framed
in the room, smaller, waits as in an album.

Light burns its nostalgia for day.
And all the darkness around lamp and table

changes to the crosshatchings of pen-and-ink sketch,
like the marks of clawing.

PHOTO OF TWO BOOMERS

> Do you imagine the universe is agitated?
> —LAO TZU

Sitting on a log outside his motorcycle
garage, Moon reaches for another Camel,
though he hasn't lit the first one yet;
Raoul, under his favorite ball cap, contemplates
where his cup of jasmine tea has gone.

Still hairy, heads like gray pom-poms,
they have almost given up the plan to take
over the world. And what's become of
their wonderful anger over the Draft? That
not turned to humor settles into congestion.

Who is taking this shot? One's daughter may
have tried to pose them or else a young friend
who sees them as cowpokes, always picturesque,
their faces the saddles of time.
Where once their universe was agitated,

now it's desert stars and night.
Like camels settling at oasis, they grin
and grunt. Like jasmine, they find enough
shade to bloom and squint into the wind
that is always hot but welcome.

TRIBAL HILLS

Though we haven't seen each other since we bounced our bicycles
down hills around town, we were in the same tribe of youth.
So I come the miles when you call, drive my gas guzzler in icy
rain to your flattened tire at the West Virginia end of Route 52,
working toward you like the mythic mail carrier of old.

There are other men and women like you I would not feel
the urge to help, would resist the pull to come where their car
had conked out and they sat alone in winter dark.

It's not the same impulse that yanks me out the door
with rain slicker, fear, flashlight, and hot coffee to aid
my daughter, but it's related.

Why you and not others I've known better and longer?
And it's not just because you called me.
I've found I can say no to about anyone, and have.

You and I never carried rifles, sat in mud, or stanched
one another's blood. We didn't write when we moved
to opposite ends of each other's lives.

But there's something invisible out there, in here.
When I step from my truck, I know only
that I have something tentative as memory of many
hillside wounded, of all lives running like one
into earth, of return to the ancient village
with one who was also worn down in these hills.

SPRING FEVER

Spring goes off, leaving me behind again.
I kept watch for that moment when trees,
Still winter bare, cracked their twig ends

And colors squirmed out. But I blinked
And they showed up as the moon
Watched. Each new leaf now is further

Into green and a block away, every blossom
Pinked and whitened and more than a mile
gone. I push my face into that of every flower

As if reverse engineering birth by smell.
I count robins as if that will remake
Me into cat. There is no holiness

Like the clear sharpness of this air.
So, I seek out first thorns to push
My finger into, letting out more red.

ONE TREE

Wherever I lived, in houses all over town,
there was always one tree

in a backyard near the wood fence
or beside a splintering porch

of my friend or almost in the center
of a vacant lot—an oak, a wide birch,

a very old maple—one that had grown
too large to fell easily, so lived on

growing rank in imagination and showing
up in dreams as a place to hide,

a tree like a pet elephant, a refuge to run to
when time threatened,

a tree with limbs like neighborhoods
to the green news above the town,

a giant free of other giants,
a tree I dragged the world into.

CROSSING NO MAN'S LAND

The fence is rustier on this side
where ownership has not tamed
corrosion. The grass feels woollier.

The bald moon shakes off its hood.
Under such illumination, my timid
flashlight shudders, and I want to hide

my shotgun, but Gonzo and Suzy
are all over some maple's trunk.
I hear their sweet baying

as a poor raccoon worries
up branches, as if in making it
to no man's land, trees are bases.

GENTLE LIFE

after dancing in the window all day from sunrise to sunset
they would sip of the tea . . .
   —JOHN CLARE

The light-touch moth larva pulling cashmere,
One-half fiber at a time, from your pink sweater
In the back of the closet, the quietly rising
Flanks of the young boar nosing for roots
In black earth, and the cat mask the night wears
       Give it all away.
The even quiet of evening, monotonous
Tisk of night beetles, chorus of locusts, hiss
Of butterfly ticks surrounding you feel
Like part of the conspiracy of the scene
      When you are at home
Where it is harder to believe in escape than habit.

FRIEND DARKNESS

(1961)

Once a year in winter, they worked
a weeklong shift, called "Midnight,"
arose like vampires at dusk,
and drove to separate factories
at 11 p.m. to return home before dawn.

Old enough to be on my own
those late and early hours, I became
a light sleeper with all house lights
on for seven nights.
Never having met you formally,

I had glimpsed you between
trees, as I ran trash out to the alley.
You were the bully I somehow avoided
on the playground.
Then the power failed

the fifth night of their shift.
I lit twin flashlights and slogged over
eight inches of moon-packed snow
to where the fuse box hid in the cellar,
like a chest of gold. Standing at stair top,

I think of you as a black
St. Bernard predictable and steady,
curled in cave warmth,
my lights stroking your dark coat
with sheen. I will walk your long body,

run through your close breath, find
the blown fuse, the switch. But first,
like the ghost from my own future,
I wish to whisper in my younger ear
how you'd save me two years hence

when a drunk uncle slinks in
looking for drink money
or something soft to penetrate
with hard disgust. How he never finds
me under your black fur.

BOTTOM OF THE WELL

(1958)

At eleven, tired of surface Earth and never
having met a well in person, I believed any
might lead to the Hell so clearly described
at our Nazarene church. I wanted no one to know
and so slipped out to the ruined farm at the end
of town looking for an entrance. I took off my shoes.
I was ready, I was not. But I trusted the Boy Scout
compass to be my guide. Though it gave only
horizontal guidance, I hung it around my neck anyway,
clipped a flashlight to my belt, tied a fifty-foot rope
to the closest hickory, clinched a jackknife in my teeth,
and shoved crates from the well top. I threw the rope in first,
dropped a penny after it. Took its "Ping, ping, ploink!"
as reassurance. Six feet down the rope, I wished
for gloves. Though the walls were dry, I could
barely get a toehold. It grew cooler toward Hell.
My little light bumped its nose against stone.
When I slipped an inch and screamed, the open knife
dove into darkness. Better, I thought, to go weaponless
into the underworld. Slickened stones bit my knees
at every turn. I neared water's level and the end
of my rope, thinking that this may be the stupidest
thing ever. I saw the well mouth floating, like a moon,
gazing straight down on my foolishness. With less
than a foot of rope and my arms weak as string,
I dropped. . . . Cold water squeezed all air and heat
from me. If I had to die, at least I'd reach my goal.
Tired of treading water, I flipped and pulled my way

down slimy walls. After all the head throbbing
and lung stinging I could bear, I prayed, I disassembled
in wavy shadow, and trapped dream water, sank in silt
to my elbows, hugged it like a pillow. Then I felt the loop
of a rope tap softly at my back. Like the Savior's hand
my grandfather always preached, he stood beside the full
halo of his flashlight, pulling me up, having heard my prayer.

SYMPATHY FOR ICE

I hear your coming like the mast bell
of an ancient freighter.

Each morning, I look for you in light
fur-frost on fallen leaves
and think of your glowing
under the blank quilt of night.

I scuff to the fridge often with a tall glass,
in my hand, your clairvoyant cousin,
and fill her with tap water
and cubes to take part in the ritual
mating and rebirth of cold.

It's almost church, almost faith, carrying
you to the last warm room.
I climb onto the bed, sit on four blankets' thickness
and stretch out like an ice crystal forming:
warmth, my cold; rest, my freezing.

Out past the dark-throttled leaves
and the clan of disappearing boulders,
the river clears its throat for your coming.
The wood frog folds into prayer.

PLAGUE DOCTOR

(Paris, 1656)

At first, just walking the street
In this waxed wool suit felt strange
As finding a loaf of bread, warm
And comfortably soft, still baking
In the ruins of a burnt house, butter
Sizzling on a nearby knife.
Now, I wouldn't recognize myself
Passing any mirror without the goggle-eyed
Snout mask (storax, cloves, ambergris, balm-
Mint leaves and other scents alive in there
Like seasonings for a stork's supper)
And the heaviness of this black outfit.
Each night just climbing into bed,
I peel the day off like a dossil bandage.
Once I'd carve on the skin of tomatoes,
Idling, waiting to sell market fruit
And now can't lift sheets or autopsy
Remains fast enough to close down the dark
Seeds routing bodies. While I sweat
Over their loved one's remains, children
Lean in the door chanting, "Doctor Beak."

ANIMAL DOLLS

What wordless song floated from their heartless
forms as they lounged on her bed, leaned at her
window seat, and slouched atop her hope chest,

each in its plastic bag? We could not know (rat
in its lace dress, pigeon in housecoat, crow
in a white cape, barn owl in blue robe, possum

in Cossack coat) to what feral gods she prayed
in her sleep. Her old rubber and porcelain
babies lay naked in a pyramid, piled

behind the garage. No longer cosseted pets.
Sometimes, early or late, as official light waxed
or waned, she'd stroll back from the longest

county road, her basket often over-filled
with those the road had thrown off, intact,
overnight—never the mashed or the mangled.

We worried like mice, knew we should do
something. Against every doctor's
prescription of confinement, we wait for her—
our only daughter's—zodiac to be complete.

MY GARDEN

This world didn't exist until
I imagined it, made it other
And gave it the name. I stretched a wire
Fence around a part of the backyard,
An idea within an idea,
And put in twelve beefsteaks. That night, I looked
Up, saw the stars like fingernail scratches
On a night glass, knew what I was doing,
Knew the universe as already grown,
Transformed. Now I can point at parts
And call each name. See what I have done,
These tall greens that grow, the stakes and wires
That hold them up like drunks, their huge reddish
Examples. They stagger, so new to this that
They've become. I should do this everywhere.

PICNIC IN THE CEMETERY

Anything we do here, except bow
heads, is out of place, yet everything
else knows exactly what to do.
                    The mourning dove
sits right on her wooden marker;
grass leans in its choir of sun.

Crows scan for cues to a burial.
Our egg salad, smoked sausages,
and basket, helpless, wait.
                    Ants do not invade
the sugar we brought for strawberries
or set one feeler on the spread quilt.

White-green lichens cling to the oldest
stones like hope to the mind.
My father's grave's a whisper away.

Your shoulders and thighs gleam
as their own kind of marble.
                    Our nudity among the dead
at once feels right, yet punishable.

WOODS GHOST

Beside the sycamore, she's blonde
as a hornet's nest, next to the elm,
dark as a lightning-struck limb. She's
forgotten the meaning of every word

and growls instead of speaks. Seeing
the light of your windows like forest
fire, she streaks from pane to pane.
Don't think to go out to her.

Even if she were just murdered,
a second of terror is endless,
so it's been forever since she felt
kind. The habit of breathing she

forsook had caused the knife to lick
deeper into her lung, the bullet to spin
one twist more into her heart. Oldest
of the wild, she's not come to be forgiven.

EVERYTHING REMAINS

2/15/13

Today, asteroid DA14 slipped past Earth
About seventeen thousand miles away,
A close call, as they say, of astronomical space.

Earlier, a meteor the size of a bus maimed
A thousand Russians. At least one hundred
Forty thousand others died of various causes,

But all I'll likely recall of this day is my sister's
Passing. I feel everything that was her remains
Down here, somewhere, except her personality.

And that is left in the electrochemical sparks
Of our family brains. She and I never did agree
On our ideas of heaven. More than anything,

I hope she has gone to hers, because all that mine
Has done is throw a couple of stones this way.

(i.m. Sharon L. Hensley, 1950–2013)

When I was a runaway, I hid
behind a small church, slid a penny
under the back door to keep it from locking
automatically.
After services, I slipped in. Old folding chairs
lay on their sides like swimmers longing
to turn from wood back to water.
The emptiness
of pews stared at the absence behind
the pulpit. I was alone, too,
just looking out into darkness
from the front door.
Encircling
the porch light, a group of midges,
gnats, and mosquitoes rehearsed
their one ritual to the cloud-covered moon.

THANKSGIVING INSECTS

All the *Agra vation* have fallen like flowers of the field.
I will not see their black-and-white, native American,
speckled legs pivot like garden gates again this year.

And the *Aha ha,* imported here by Mr. Menke,
have fled the neighborhood. One of the last
this season stung him, in waspish fashion, helping
to roll his Morris Minor into a drainage culvert.

Carmenelectra shechisme, tiniest of the moths
that flutter about the porch, not one has ever
seen a second summer. Nothing left of them
but wing powder, before November breezes,
fallen, less than leaf dust, like memory
of all gone autumns. But it is the little red spider,

Calponia harrisonfordi, out for adventure on the underside
of every other leaf . . . after he disappears, there's no
heart to the season, nothing to lure the birds of winter
out to do their leaf-turning dance. Only the plague hours
of emptiness till the first snowman glows at the night edge
of porch light, waving good-bye, sinking back into earth.

RENDEZVOUS

Why do you walk so often at evening,
out the back door, stroll across the grass,

down to the fence and the back gate, just
to stand gazing at darkness brewing

in the line of firs and the whispering
of winds among thousands of needles,

rough and flaking bark, thick pillow
of fallen leaves, and tightfisted

pine cones, as if at the shoreline
of night and the sand of day, skin

after skin of hours coming
down, layering, as if to lean

there waiting to meet it, gossip
with it, the life behind the life.

PHANTOM FLESH

My great-aunt's great arms
were seismic slabs I feared.
Passing near their cetaceous wobble,

I smelled bleach and sea breeze.
When she lifted them to hang
wet sheets on her clothesline,

I expected to see loose droops ooze
to fleshy drops. Bewitched, I
stared in moonlight at chicken

necks lined up on her chopping
stump. I saw those arms go down
where crawdads rattle claws in clear

or murky shore. I tear up now
remembering her and what comes
from the wear and the blue of time's pull.

THE INNOCENCE OF FEET

I uncover yours for watching while you sleep.
They know your weight, have no idea
of Earth as the moveable shape they hold.

They dream, twitching over hot sand,
tickling beneath trees, pine needles
making them tiptoe and stub.

On the floor like a fetishist, I watch your feet retell
of carrying you spring to winter. I love that
they say nothing about nine months

in a weightless room with nothing to dream,
awaiting the burden their arches imply.
Mirror twins, everywhere together,

troubled sleeping apart, exposed on moonlit sheets,
they drift toward each other as if murmuring
the impossibility of running alone.

Regretting years spent clasped in leather, canvas,
rubber—wet leaves missed the most—
they know living, the affair of miles.

DOGS WAITING

Coming home late, down the alley,
I'd howl and become surrounded
by a chorus of yips and yowls to cover
my lateness. The way they'd sit out
in evening fields, on corners, or in backyards,
like a choir, listening beyond the whir
of mosquitoes and hiss of streetlamps
for distant sirens was communion.
If they heard no siren wailing sorrow,
no moon clarifying distance, they still had stars.

I wonder, if they took such twinkling
whiteness to be snow out of season,
tree-caught before landing, or the tiny,
pale blossoms of the blackest mythic tree
no canine had ever sniffed the trunk
or the roots of. And I wonder, is this
how all beings once handled the impatience
of longing? On mid-July nights, hounds
and terriers divided indoors, our setter
still waits, muzzle through curtains,
solemn, sharing the solitude of the street.

THE PERFECT WINDOW

Now it looms, lambent, rectangular,
four-paned, and suspended in shadow where I see it
at evening across the street. Gradually, the prosaic
weight of watching matches the darkening air, the poetic
stillness of space.

When dwellers behind their window turn
off the light, night becomes general, a memory of memory,
no particular recalling of *What was that hovering idea
of illumination? Bright place of elsewhere?
Reflection in night's eye?*

From my imperfect window,
I study night winds, remembering where fireflies have
winked like local stars, count the steps from this planet
to that across the street, contemplate the patient hosannas
of trees.

A passing night-walker slogs by, down to sleep.
Out of respect for the other's odyssey, we do not wave or speak.

THE WAY THINGS WAIT

In attic or basement, boxes
wait to be filled with rusted hammers
or remain to be cleared of iron nails
and broken into kindling.

Jars linger to be empty of all but air,
free of their relish,
pickles, or beets.

A trunk stands until opened, cleared
of folded tablecloths, embroidered shirts,
and ornaments once known to hang.

Festoons of dust and filigree of cobwebs
pause till air wings them off or they fall
like tired angels.

Baskets pose, elegance of grass and reed,
packed bottom to top with clean clothes
towed each Sunday from the dryer.

Sleds and dress dummies take side trips
upstairs to return scraped or frayed
at the end of their seasons.

Things holding their places for hours
or years in the disappearing alchemy of form.
Their only prospect the same as ours,
dissolution, intimacy with atom.

MY SISTER'S GHOST

She stands in the dark of the closet,
As in a forest, but will come when I call—

Not a pet lying by the fireplace,
Waiting for me to look her way.

But she will drift closer
As I feel around for her life

In something like stars reflected
In rainwater. Then she drifts

To the long hallway of sleep, to wait
For the right dream to begin.

I keep trying to believe
She has just moved to another

Florida, even brighter than the one
Where she lived for so long.

In this one, she should be happy,
Even find her lost childhood,

The one she remembered
Nothing of and I remember all

Of our fights and arguments.
A little tomboy, stealing my clothes,

She stands in the dark closet,
Still lost in one of my shirts.

EILEEN STEPS DOWN INTO THE CELLAR

Through the semidarkness at the edge of her flashlight
beam to retrieve six potatoes for winter dinner, lumpy
weird veggies easy to make into almost anything,
originally from, some say, all the way out in the Andes,
wherever that is, potatoes that her family crew grew
and stacked in the backmost, highest corner in July heat,
sunlight landing like a cut wedge of cheddar right
out of the air over this very floor, now so dark,

where she squishes a cricket fat enough her foot
slides for a second, her flashlight meteoric then silent,
and she tumbles into this absurd endless dark—
all darkness being endless when you are lost in it—
and insect waste and debris. An alien environment
right here, under her house, and just below her kitchen.

DREAM GEOGRAPHY

In mine, scrub trees
fail to climb abrupt slopes, people cling
with pitons, ice axes, and blur of words. Mountains, as if hollow,

echo old songs. Nightly, I dream of Laloya and Wigman. I named them
at eight. In Himalayan dream light, they keep vigil over sleep,
on peaks higher than tree line or air,

one spirit watching another. Like snowman and snow leopard, only they know
if each other still exists. Yet, I dream them still, squinting at wind,
watching my ascent through sparks of snow.

AN AUTO MECHANIC CONSIDERING SNOW

Decked out like a Chrysler Imperial,
winter has slapped on its white sidewalls
and hit the road for the first show.

Or fifty thousand angels tumbled out
of the bus to Heaven and crashed head-on
into lawns, leaving only the slush

of white feathers all over town. Early
sun turns into chrome on snowfields and streets.
The few spots of earth not covered show

like rust. Wind revs its engine across
the flats of December. On this short walk,
Sunday air is gasoline in the lungs,

but the joyrider in me doesn't care.
I am the top-down, happy-dog sitting
shotgun with nothing ahead but horizon.

FIRST INSOMNIA

What you gain on the hobbyhorse, you lose on the swings.
—AN ADAGE

I was thirteen. I should have loved it
for opening up new curtained rooms
of night, but I had too much enjoyed
tumbling into sleep with no concern
for how I landed in unconsciousness,
as if it were a backyard trampoline.

The featurelessness puberty of night was on me
then as I lay there wild awake for endless
hours of now. No demarcation like morning
to make sense of the map of time, I stared
at the ceiling, adrift, losing everything
or walking the listing deck, window

to window, of rudderless ship.
After so long, daylight becomes paint,
shellac on darkness. Life, a myth,
loses its meaning, like that country we
may visit, perhaps Italy, somewhere
in our lost youth to come.

DREAM OF THREE LIONS

The soul remembers the beauty it used to know in Heaven.
— *KNIGHT OF CUPS*

For some reason, hammering piano, whining
violins, scratching guitars play as three lions
pad onto the desert and flop matter-of-factly
among date palms, their world unsliced by bars.

Every second of my dream, I cause the trillions
of sand grains to be here, to stay here, decide
the size of oasis trees, the degree of slope,
the absence of breeze, and instruments that play,

but whether these lions are guides, destroyers,
neither, makes me want to run beyond the nothingness
of sleep, the selfishness of dream. Now, midnight
sky the right darkness of blue, I don't know where

clouds may be, but the cotton of light is everywhere.
The wide spray of stars, the honesty of moon, tell me
that in any of three yawning mouths, under this drench
of dry air, I may find morning and what's to remember.

TO MAKE A THING

I was too young to be trusted alone
in that much water, and we were too poor
to use much more, so Mother bathed
me between her legs. My first
and last memory of being close to her
is in that claw-foot tub. Her quick, soapy
hands, large hanging breasts, clay-colored
nipples—how much is memory, how much
Oedipal fantasy? The red triangle of her groin
filled me with dread and a wild curiosity.
As the soap broke down to liquid to make
its foam in her hands that cleansed
my cellophane skin, I had no idea how
my mind would work to fracture events,
rebuilding them as memory. When I think
of her as she was the next forty years shredding
old cardboard onto the factory floor for
a brown snowfall that made pulp for the next
generation of boxes, the way she shouted
at me through her new apartment door to go
back to her mother's house so she could get
sleep for the next shift, or backhanded me
when I irritated her—all that broke my imbecile
heart and gave me license to be the adventurer
I turned into, breaking the bones that kept
me tractioned in bed learning to read and love
the poetry, the stories, time to imagine and over-
think, to chart the land of metaphor—I have to
thank her now for all the neglect, for teaching me
to make a thing, you have to break a thing.

NIGHT ANGEL

I was stoned, but he was old, between Einstein
and Richard Harris for the long white hair,
surprising for an angel. He showed up,

like a chicken hawk, behind me, where I leaned
against the chimney smoking, late one night.
I was just tired and frayed enough to say I wanted

to jump to that turret on the nearest Victorian house
down the block. He said something about not being
my wishing lamp, but we hopped there anyhow.

Suddenly, I felt it must be a scene from *The Divine Comedy*
or Ezekiel 2 of the Bible, something covertly alien.
From the start I knew in my marrow what he was.

He felt common and necessary, like a twin or cellmate.
"Who was the first," I asked, squatting on the stones,
"to leap to the idea of God when they beheld you?"

HOME MOVIE

(after Julia Kasdorf)

In the home movie that runs endlessly through my head,
there's a part that gets stuck each time where the camera pans
around past the reupholstered chair, over the three-legged table
propped in the corner, the red scarf hiding the missing leg,
beyond the dusty window through which I see all the way down to
the tobacco barn, to the field beyond, and back into the living room
of the old Lane house, and you are not there.

This is the part I cannot stand to see another time,
where I would re-edit and have you in the chair,
that you skinned and reskinned, or have you setting a bowl
of the faded wax fruit you like on the table as if apologizing
for kicking one of its legs off and throwing it at Jack, our blue-tick,
for eating the eggs you spilled onto the stone floor;
or I would have you on the tractor coming out of the barn

that day you sold the whole crop in town, that other happy day,
before you let the curses fly like the red words of Jesus, and your man
ran off and took whatever it was of yourself you had given him,
leaving only the sprung and rusted parts, those that became stand-ins
for mother and what you thought of yourself. I want to go around the room
and pet each thing that is a creature of this film—you, Jack, the table,
and the broken leg still under it—and say, "It's okay," as if we could rewind.

TWILIGHT IN THE CEMETERY

A stray dog trots, looking at me over his shoulder—a slight breeze—
    two crows
sidestepping on a limb above the tallest mausoleum.

Static air quickens. Leaves shake. The smell of dust, first heavy drops
splatter against marble and granite.

The valley shows teeth, takes a breath, holds it: the first blare of
    lightning.
Orchestral thunder. The opera begins. A gothic aria

tumbles out of each cloud. Hills and headstones shudder, phase in,
    out—
all the light darkness can register.

Everything staggers, black and white. Only the land does not move.
The dead can't rise. Electrons linger

and quake, thickening ether. A white thing, a human couple, naked,
    interlocked
arms and legs, rolls behind a tombstone thick as a castle wall.

Clear epitaphs of rain carve air. I put my camera away. Disappearing
    between flashes,
Earth turns ancient and strange again.

www.ingramcontent.com/pod-product-compliance
Lightning Source LLC
Chambersburg PA
CBHW022154090426
42742CB00010B/1506